Cataraqui United Church Cemetery 6

The Grave Whisperer

Angeline Gallant

Published by Angeline Gallant, 2022.

While every precaution has been taken in the preparation of this book, the publisher assumes no responsibility for errors or omissions, or for damages resulting from the use of the information contained herein.

CATARAQUI UNITED CHURCH CEMETERY 6

First edition. November 20, 2022.

Copyright © 2022 Angeline Gallant.

ISBN: 979-8215663776

Written by Angeline Gallant.

Also by Angeline Gallant

A Dragon's Diary
Dreaming of Dragons

Calling Her Heart
Whisper of the Heart
No Turning Back
Forsake Me Not
Hear My Cry
Calling Her Heart Boxed Set Volumes 1-4

FORGET ME NOT
Victoria, Ontario's Babies 1894 - 1895

Keeper Of Secrets
A Lady's Secret

Midnight's Awakening

Heart of the Storm
Walking Through The Storm
Midnight's Awakening boxed set volumes 1-3

Secrets of the Underworld
Deklan's Dragons
Secrets of the Underworld Volumes 1 & 2

Tell My Story Collection
Tell My Story: England 1852

The Grave Whisperer
Wedding Bells in Kingston, Ontario, Canada 1923
St. Paul's Anglican Churchyard Kingston, Ontario, Canada A-B
St. Paul's Anglican Churchyard, Kingston, Ontario, Canada C - D
St. Paul's Anglican Churchyard, Kingston, Ontario, Canada G - H
St. Paul's Anglican Churchyard, Kingston, Ontario, Canada J - N
St. Paul's Anglican Churchyard, Kingston, Ontario, Canada O - R
St. Paul's Anglican Churchyard, Kingston, Ontario, Canada S - T
St. Paul's Anglican Churchyard, Kingston, Ontario T - Z
Small Graveyards & Burial Grounds: Kingston, Ontario, Canada
Cataraqui United Church Cemetery 1
Cataraqui United Church Cemetery 2
Cataraqui United Church Cemetary 3
Cataraqui United Church Cemetery 4
Cataraqui United Church Cemetery 5
Beth Israel Cemetery
Cataraqui United Church Cemetery 6

Table of Contents

FRANCIS GUESS[1]

Francis was born in Johnstown, New York in 1813. He was Irish.

He was 29 years old when his daughter, Harriet, ws born in 1842.

Francis was 31 years old when his son, James Sidney, was born in 1844.

He was 38 years old when his father passed away in 1851.

Francis was 39 years old when his son, Barnabas Secord, was born in 1852.

He was 41 years old when his daughter, Calista Ann, was born in 1854.

Francis was 46 years old when his daughter, Victoria, was born in 1859.

He was 49 years old when his mother and brother, Edward, passed away in 1862.

Francis was 50 years old when his daughter, Permilla, was born in 1863.

He was 67 years old when his wife passed away in 1880.

Francis was 77 years old when the Women's Suffrage Movement began in 1890.

He was 81 years old when he passed away on January 22, 1894. Francis was Methodist.

JAMES GUESS[2]

James passed away on January 25, 1852.

HANNAH MARY HALL[3]

Hannah was born on March 15, 1860.

She passed away just before her first birthday on March 9, 1861.

HENRY LLOYD HANSEN[4]

Henry was born on October 3, 1891. He was German.

He was nine years old when his sister, Edna Alberta, passed away in 1901.

Henry was 14 years old when Ontario Hydro was established in 1906.

He was 15 years old when his father passed away in 1907.

Henry was 42 years old when the Dionne Quintuplets were born in 1934.

He was 43 years old when his mother passed away in 1935.

Henry was 54 years old when his sister, Lena May, passed away in 1946.

He was 58 years old when his brother, George Frederick, passed away in 1950.

Henry was 62 years old when his brother, William David, passed away in 1954.

He was 73 years old when his brother, James Stanley, passed away in 1965.

Henry was 81 years old when his brother, Otto Victor, passed away January 16, 1973. He passed away three days later on January 9th. Henry was Methodist.

HORACE ADAMS HARBACK[5]

Horace was born in the United States on February 19, 1840.

He was 22 years old when the Battle of Gettysburg took place in 1863.

Horace was 30 years old when British Columbia joined the confederation in 1871.

He was 47 years old when he passed away on January 3, 1888.

AGNES (HOWIE) HARPELL[6]

Agnes was born in Frontenac, Ontario on March 3, 1874. She was Scottish.

She was eight years old when the mining boom in northern Ontario began in 1883.

Agnes was 23 years old when she married Charles Wesley in Frontenac, Ontario on December 22, 1897.

She was 26 years old when her father passed away in 1900.

Agnes was 27 years old when her daughter, Janet Alma, was born in 1901.

She was 30 years old when her son, Westford, was born in 1904.

Agnes was 31 years old when Ontario Hydro was established in 1906.

She was 32 years old when her daughter, Mary, was born on December 23, 1906. Mary passed away on June 30, 1907.

Agnes was 35 years old when her mother passed away in 1909.

She was 38 years old when her daughter, Selma Agnes, was born in 1913.

Agnes was 58 years old when her brother, James, passed away in 1933.

She was 59 years old when the Dionne Quintuplets were born in 1934.

Agnes was 72 years old when her brother, Archibald, passed away in 1947.

She was 76 years old when she passed away in Frontenac, Ontario in February 1951. Agnes is buried in Kingston, Ontario. She was Methodist.

THOMAS ALBERT "BERT" HARPELL[7]

Thomas was born in 1868. He was German.

He was three years old when British Columbia joined the confederation in 1871.

Thomas was 15 years old when the mining boom in northern Ontario began in 1883.

He was 24 years old when his brother, William, passed away in 1892.

Thomas was 28 years old and working as a gardener when he passed away on August 3, 1896. He was Methodist.

CHARLES WESLEY "WESLEY" HARPELL[8]

Wesley was born in 1871. He was German.

He was 11 years old when the mining boom in northern Ontario began in 1883.

Wesley was 18 years old when the Women's Suffrage movement began in 1890.

He was 21 years old when his brother, William, passed away in 1892.

Wesley was 25 years old when his brother, Thomas Albert, passed away in 1896.

He was 26 years old when he married Agnes in Frontenac, Ontario on December 22, 1897.

Wesley was 30 years old when his daughter, Janet Alma, was born in 1901.

He was 33 years old when his son, Wesford, was born in 1904.

Wesley was 35 years old when his daughter, Mary, was born in 1906. She passed away less than a year later.

He was 41 years old when his daughter, Selma Agnes, was born in 1913.

Wesley was 43 years old when his father passed away in 1914.

He was 58 years old when his sister, Emily Jane, passed away in 1929.

Wesley was 60 years old when his mother passed away in 1931.

He was 67 years old when his sister, Effie May, passed away in 1939.

Wesley was 79 years old when his wife and sister, Agnes, both passed away in February 1951.

He was 83 years old when his sister, Martha Lavina, passed away in 1954.

Wesley was 88 years old when he passed away in 1959. He was Methodist.

FLOYD J. HARPELL[9]

Floyd was an infant when he passed away. His birthdate and date of death are currently unknown.

JOHN HENRY HARPELL[10]

John was born in 1836. He was German.

He was 24 years old when his daughter, Emily Jane, was born in 1860.

John was 26 years old when his daughter, Anna Alzina, was born in 1863.

He was 29 years old when his brother, Samuel, passed away in 1866.

John was 30 years old when his daughter, Martha Lavina, was born in 1866.

He was 30 years old when Ontario was founded on July 1, 1867.

John was 31 years old when his son, Thomas Albert, was born in 1868.

He was 33 years old when his father passed away in 1869.

John was 34 years old when his son, Charles Wesley, was born in 1871.

He was 37 years old when his daughter, Annie Roxanna, was born in 1874.

John was 42 years old when his son, Willet Roy, was born in 1879.

He was 46 years old when his mother passed away in 1883.

John was 48 years old when his daughter, Effie May, was born in 1885.

He was 55 years old when his son, William, passed away in 1892.

John was 60 years old when his son, Thomas Albert, passed away in 1896.

He was 69 years old when Ontario Hydro was established in 1906.

John was 71 years old when his sister, Julia Ann, passed away in 1907.

He was 75 years old when his brother, Henry, passed away in 1912.

John was 76 years old when his brother, Jacob Barlet, passed away in 1913.

He was 78 years old when he passed away in 1914. John was Methodist and a farmer.

MARIE HARPELL[11]

Marie was an infant when she passed away. At this time, little else is known.

MARTHA LAVINA HARPELL[12]

Martha was born in 1866.

She was a year old when Ontario was founded on July 1, 1867.

Martha was 15 years old when the Chinese Exclusion Act was passed in 1882.

She was 16 years old when the mining boom in northern Ontario began in 1883.

Martha was 25 years old when her brother, William, passed away in 1892.

She was 29 years old when her brother, Thomas Albert, passed away in 1896.

Martha was 46 years old when the Central Banking System was established in 1913.

She was 48 years old when her father passed away in 1914.

Martha was 63 years old when her sister, Emily Jane, passed away in 1929.

She was 72 years old when her sister, Effie May, passed away in 1939.

Martha was 84 years old when her sister, Annie Roxanna, passed away in 1951.

She was 87 years old when she passed away on July 16, 1954. Martha was German and Methodist.

MARY ANN (JOHNSON) HARPELL[13]

Mary was born in 1840.

She was 17 years old when her son, William, was born in 1858.

Mary was 20 years old when her daughter, Emily Jane, was born in 1860.

She was 22 years old when her daughter, Anna Alzina, was born in 1863.

Mary was 26 years old when her daughter, Martha Lavina, was born in 1866.

She was 26 years old when Ontario was founded on July 1, 1867.

Mary was 27 years old when her son, Thomas Albert, was born in 1868.

She was 30 years old when British Columbia joined the confederation in 1871.

Mary was 31 years old when her son, Charles Wesley, was born in 1871.

She was 33 years old when her daughter, Annie Roxanna, was born in 1874.

Mary was 42 years old when the mining boom in northern Ontario began in 1883.

She was 44 years old when her daughter, Effie May, was born in 1885.

Mary was 52 years old when her son, William, passed away in 1892.

She was 56 years old when her son, Thomas Albert, passed away in 1896.

Mary was 65 years old when Ontario Hydro was established in 1906.

She was 89 years old when her daughter, Emily Jane, passed away in 1929.

Mary was 91 years old when she passed away in 1931. She was German and Methodist.

MARY MITCHELL JOHNSTON HARPELL[14]

Mary was born on December 23, 1906. She passed away on June 30, 1907.

WILLIAM H. HARPELL[15]

William was born in 1859.

He was eight years old when Ontario was founded on July 1, 1867.

William was 12 years old when British Columbia joined the confederation in 1871.

He was 24 years old when the mining boom of northern Ontario began in 1883.

William was 29 years old when he married Mary in Kingston, Ontario on May 3, 1888.

He was 31 years old when his son, Herbert Wellington, was born in 1890.

William was 33 years old when he passed away on April 6, 1892. He was German, Methodist and a laborer.

HENRY HARPELL[16]

Henry was born in 1806.

He was 27 years old when his son, Henry, was born in 1833.

Henry was 29 years old when his daughter, Nancy, was born in 1835.

He was 30 years old when his son, John Henry, was born in 1836.

Henry was 38 years old when his father passed away in 1844.

He was 48 years old when his sister, Margaret, passed away in 1854.

Henry was 56 years old when his sister, Elizabeth Jane, passed away in 1862.

He was 60 years old when his son, Samuel, passed away in 1866.

Henry was 61 years old when Ontario was established on July 1, 1867.

He was 63 years old when he passed away in 1869.

NATHANIEL S. HATCH[17]

Nathaniel was a War of 1812 veteran.
He passed away on May 8, 1857.

MADELINE HAYES[18]

Madeline was born in 1953.

She was 29 years old when the Canada Act was passed in 1982.

Madeline was 67 years old when she passed away in 2020.

ANNA HENDERSON[19]

Anna was born in 1879.

She was four years old when the mining boom in northern Ontario began in 1883.

Anna was 85 years old when she passed away in 1964.

GEORGE HENDERSON[20]

George was born in 1872.

He was 11 years old when the mining boom in northern Ontario began in 1883.

George was 85 years old when he passed away in 1957.

JAMES HENDERSON[21]

James passed away on March 10, 1849.

JANE (MURRAY) HENDERSON[22]

Jane was born in Scotland in 1790.

She was 59 years old when her husband passed away in 1849.

Jane was 77 years old when Ontario was founded on July 1, 1867.

She was 81 years old when British Columbia joined the confederation in 1871.

Jane was 86 years old when she passed away on July 22, 1876.

AGNES HENDRY[23]

To date, it is uncertain when Agnes was born or passed away.

KENNETH FENWICK HENDRY[24]

Kenneth was born in Scotland in April 1860.

He was six years old when his father passed away in 1866.

Kenneth was 20 years old when his brother, Robert John, passed away in 1881.

He was 28 years old when he married Bernice in Grinnell, Iowa on July 5, 1888.

Kenneth was 30 years old when his daughter, Doris, was born in 1890.

He was 39 years old and living in Riverside, California in 1900. At that time, he was listed as single while living with his mother and a servant.

Kenneth was 41 years old when his mother passed away in 1902.

He was 77 years old when his wife passed away in 1937.

Kenneth was 80 years old when he passed away on July 7, 1940. His brother, William, passed away the same year. Kenneth is buried in Kingston, Ontario.

ROBERT JOHN HENDRY[25]

Robert was born in Kingston, Ontario in 1861. He was Scottish.

He was five years old when his father passed away in 1866.

Robert was 10 years old when British Columbia joined the confederation in 1871.

He was 20 years old and a student when he passed away on June 10, 1881. Robert was a Congregationalist.

THOMAS HENDRY SR.[26]

Thomas was born in 1814.

He was 29 years old when "A Christmas Carol" was first published in 1843.

Thomas was 32 years old when his son, James Anderson, was born in 1846.

He was 34 years old when his daughter, Agnes, was born in 1848.

Thomas was 36 years old when his son, Thomas, was born in 1850.

He was 38 years old when his son, William Durie, was born in 1852.

Thomas was 41 years old when his daughter, Anna, was born in 1855.

He was 46 years old when his son, Kenneth Fenwick, was born in 1860.

Thomas was 47 years old when his son, Robert John, was born in 1861.

He was 52 years old when he passed away in 1866.

EFFIE MAY (HARPELL) HENRY[27]

Effie was born in 1884.

She was eight years old when her brother, William, passed away in 1892.

Effie was 12 years old when her brother, Thomas Albert, passed away in 1896.

She was 21 years old when she married William in Frontenac, Ontario on August 9, 1905.

Effie was 22 years old when Ontario Hydro was established in 1906.

She was 25 years old when her son, Chester Bogart Roy, was born in 1909.

Effie was 29 years old when her daughter, Norma Audrey, was born in 1913.

She was 30 years old when her father passed away in 1914.

Effie was 32 years old when her daughter, Geraldine, was born in 1915.

She was 37 years old when her son, Robert William Garth, was born in 1921.

Effie was 38 years old when her daughter, Geraldine, passed away in 1922. Geraldine was seven years old.

She was 42 years old when her son, Jack, was born in 1926.

Effie was 45 years old when her sister, Emily Jane, passed away in 1929.

She was 47 years old when her mother passed away in 1930.

Effie was 49 years old when she passed away in 1933. She was German and Methodist.

GERALDINE B. HENRY[28]

Geraldine was born in Kingston on December 28, 1915.
She was six years old when she passed away on October 31, 1922.

WILLIAM HENRY[29]

William was born on August 17, 1885 in Pittsburgh, Ontario. He was 16 years old when his brother, Hugh, passed away in 1901.

William was 23 years old when his son, Chester Bogart Roy, was born in 1909.

He was 24 years old when the Mann Act was passed in 1910.

William was 27 years old when his daughter, Norma Audrey, was born in 1913.

He was 29 years old when his mother passed away in 1914.

William was 30 years old when his father passed away on June 26, 1915. His daughter, Geraldine, was born on December 28th.

He was 36 years old when his son, Robert William Garth, was born in 1921.

William was 37 years when his daughter, Geraldine, passed away on October 31, 1922. She was six years old.

He was 40 years old when his son, Jack, was born in 1926.

William was 41 years old when his brother, Robert, passed away in 1927.

He was 47 years old when his wife passed away in 1933.

William was 48 years old when his sister, Ellen, passed away in 1934.

He was 50 years old when his sister, Elizabeth Ann, passed away in 1935.

William was 55 years old when his brother, David, passed away in 1940.

He was 57 years old when his sister, Mary Jane, passed away in 1942.

William was 59 years old when his son, Robert, passed away in 1944.

He was 60 years old when his brother, John, passed away in 1945.

William was 65 years old when his sister, Sarah, passed away in 1950.

He was 71 years old when his brother, Thomas Chester Bell, passed away in 1957.

William was 82 years old when his sister, Maude Evelyn, passed away in 1968.

He was 84 years old when he passed away in 1970. William was Irish and Methodist.

CHARLOTTE (PURDY) HERCHMER[30]

Charlotte was born in 1773.

She was four years old when her father passed away in 1778.

Charlotte was 17 years old when her daughter, Mary Catherine, was born in 1791.

She was 20 years old when her daughter, Charlotte, was born in 1794.

Charlotte was 36 years old when her husband passed away in 1809.

She was 39 years old when her mother passed away in 1812.

Charlotte was 57 years old when her daughter, Mary Catherine, passed away in 1831.

She was 58 years old when her sister, Catherine, passed away in 1832.

Charlotte was 63 years old when her sister, Mercy, passed away in 1837.

She was 65 years old when her brother, David, passed away in 1839.

Charlotte was 70 years old when she passed away on August 13, 1843.

NICHOLAS HERCHMER[31]

Nicholas was born on January 24, 1771. He was christened in Palatine, New York on January 27th.

He was eight years old when his brother, George, passed away in 1779.

Nicholas was 20 years old when his daughter, Mary Catherine, was born in 1791.

He was 24 years old when his father passed away in 1795.

Nicholas was 33 years old when his brother, Jacob, passed away in 1804.

He was 34 years old when his mother passed away in 1805.

Nicholas was 36 years old when the Atlantic slave trade was abolished in 1808. His sister, Maria, passed away the same year.

He was 37 years old when he passed away in 1809.

GLADYS IRENE (McKEGG) HEYMAN[32]

Gladys was born in Kingston, Ontario on July 25, 1899. She was Scottish.

She was six years old when Ontario Hydro was established in 1906.

Gladys was 20 years old when she married Franklin in Kingston, Ontario on September 22, 1919.

She was 34 years old when the Dionne Quintuplets were born in 1934.

Gladys was 56 years old when her sister, Catherine Jane, passed away in 1956.

She was 63 years old when she passed away in 1963. Gladys was Anglican.

EMILY J. (SMITH) HICKS[33]

Emily was born in 1862.

She was five years old when Ontario was founded on July 1, 1867.

Emily was nine years old when British Columbia joined the confederation in 1871.

She was 21 years old when the mining boom in northern Ontario began in 1883.

Emily was 34 years old when her father passed away in 1896.

She was 44 years old when Ontario Hydro was established in 1906.

Emily was 58 years old when she married David Roblin Hicks in Lennox and Addington, Ontario on September 9, 1920.

She was 72 years old when her brother, George Wright, passed away in 1934.

Emily was 79 years old when she passed away in 1941. She was Methodist.

HERBERT HOGAN[34]

Herbert passed away in 1878.

WILLIAM H. HOGAN[35]

William was born in 1844.

He was 23 years old when Ontario was founded on July 1, 1867.

William was 27 years old when British Columbia joined the confederation in 1871.

He was 70 years old when he passed away in 1914.

CATHERINE (McMILLAN) HORNING[36]

Catherine was born in Loughborough, Ontario in 1821.

She was 22 years old when "A Christmas Carol" was first published.

Catherine was 46 years old when Ontario was founded on July 1, 1867.

She was 74 years old when she passed away on July 1, 1895.

GEORGE B. HORNING[37]

George was born in Kingston, Ontario on November 16, 1814. He was 21 years old when his daughter, Catherine, was born in 1836.

George was 36 years old when his sister, Lena, passed away in 1851.

He was 39 years old when his wife passed away in 1854.

George was 41 years old when his mother passed away in 1856.

He was 44 years old when his father and sister, Catherine ,passed away in 1859.

George was 56 years old when British Columbia joined the confederation in 1871.

He was 73 years old when his sister, Margaret, passed away in 1888.

George was 80 years old when his wife, Catherine, passed away in 1895.

He was 84 years old when his sister, Nancy Ann, passed away in 1899.

George was 85 years old when his brother, Richard, passed away in 1900.

He was 91 years old when Ontario Hydro was established in 1906.

George was 92 years old when he passed away in Kepler, Ontario on February 20, 1907. He was German and Methodist.

JOHN P. HORNING[38]

John was born in 1855.

He was 12 years old when Ontario was founded on July 1, 1867.

John was 16 years old when British Columbia joined the confederation in 1871.

He was 22 years old when he married Sarah in Newbury, Ontario on December 20, 1877.

John was 42 years old when he passed away on April 29, 1897.

LARGRET MARGARET HORNING[39]

Largret passed away on September 19, 1856 in Kingston, Frontenac, Canada West, British Colonial America.

MARGARET J. (IRVINE) HORNING[40]

Margaret was born on May 19, 1817.

She was 42 years old when she married Richard in Frontenac, Ontario on March 19, 1860.

Margaret was 49 years old when Ontario was founded on July 1, 1867.

She was 53 years old when British Columbia joined the confederation in 1871.

Margaret was 65 years old when the mining boom in northern Ontario began in 1883.

She was 68 years old when she passed away on April 17, 1886. Margaret was Irish and Methodist.

MARY (McMILLEN) HORNING[41]

Mary passed away on September 28, 1851.

POLLY (CRANSTON) HORNING[42]

Polly was born on September 23, 1812.

She was 19 years old when her son, Abraham, was born in 1832.

Polly was 20 years old when she married Richard in 1833.

She was 21 years old when her daughter, Margaret Ann, was born in 1834.

Polly was 27 years old when her son, George, was born in 1840.

She was 38 years old when her father was born in 1851.

Polly was 46 years old when she passed away on April 10, 1859.

RICHARD HORNING[43]

Richard was born in Germany on March 3, 1809.

He was 23 years old when he married Polly Ann on July 24, 1833.

Richard was 47 years old when his mother passed away in 1856.

He was 50 years old when his father passed away on April 6, 1859. His wife passed away on April 10th. Richard's sister, Catherine, passed away on May 13th.

Richard was 51 years old when he married Margaret Irvine in Frontenac, Ontario on March 19, 1860.

He was 61 years old when British Columbia joined the confederation in 1871.

Richard was 77 years old when his wife passed away in 1886.

He was 79 years old when his sister, Margaret, passed away in 1888.

Richard was 90 years old when his sister, Nancy Ann, passed away in 1899.

He was 91 years old when he passed away on May 31, 1900.

RICHARD HORNING[44]

Richard passed away on April 6, 1859. He was married to Largret.

PHEOBE M. (BENJAMIN) HOWARD[45]

Phoebe was born in approximately 1843.
She passed away after 1881. Phoebe was Methodist.

RUSSELL HOWARD[46]

Russell was born in 1841.

He was 23 years old when his son, William, was born in 1864.

Russell was 24 years old when his daughter, Ena, was born in 1865.

He was 26 years old when his daughter, Alice Estella, was born in 1867.

Russell was 29 years old when his daughter, Lilley, was born in 1870.

He was 30 years old when British Columbia joined the confederation in 1871.

Russell was 31 years old when his son, Herbert, was born in 1872.

He was 33 years old when his daughter, Ada, was born in 1874.

Russell was 36 years old when his son, Frank, was born in 1877.

He was 38 years old when his daughter, Mabel May, was born in 1879.

Russell was 42 years old when the mining boom in northern Ontario began in 1883.

He was Methodist and a farmer.

CATHERINE (CONNOR) HOWE[47]

Catherine was 26 years old when she passed away in Kingston, Frontenac, Upper Canada, British Colonial America on July 17, 1820.

MARGARETGEN (VanORDEN) HOWE [48]

Margaretgen was christened in 1752 in either New York or New Jersey in a Lutheran church.

She is buried in Kingston, Ontario.

MARGARET (GALLOWAY) HOWE[49]

Margaret passed away on February 12, 1868.

MATTHEW HOWE[50]

Matthew was born in New York Colony on May 29, 1774. He was christened in New York, New York, on May 3, 1775.

Matthew was 15 years old when his mother passed away in 1790.

He was 31 years old when his sister, Elizabeth, passed away in 1805.

Matthew was 33 years old when the Atlantic slave trade was abolished in 1808.

He was 34 years old when he married Margaret in 1808.

Matthew was 45 years old when his brother, William, passed away in 1820.

He was 50 years old when his brother, Daniel, passed away in 1825.

Matthew was 71 years old when his brother, George, passed away in 1846.

He was 81 years old when he passed away on March 16, 1856.

WILLIAM HOWE[51]

William was born in 1750. He was a Loyalist.
He was 40 years old when his wife passed away in 1790.
William was 44 years old when he passed away in 1794.

ELIZA (BENNETT) HOWES[52]

Eliza was born in 1818.

She was 22 years old when her son, George, was born in 1840.

Eliza was 24 years old when her son, Thomas, was born in 1842.

She was 33 years old when her son, William, was born in 1851.

Eliza was 43 years old when her daughter, Eliza was born in 1861.

She was 49 years old when Ontario was founded on July 1, 1867.

Eliza was 52 years old when her son, Thomas, passed away in 1870.

She was 59 years old when her daughter, Eliza, passed away in 1877. Eliza was 16 years old.

Eliza was 64 years old when her husband passed away in 1882.

She was 65 years old when the mining boom in northern Ontario began in 1883.

Eliza was 68 years old when she passed away in Parham, Ontario in 1886. She is buried in Kingston, Ontario.

GEORGE HOWES[53]

George was born in Ireland in 1804.

He was 41 years old when the Irish Potato Famine took place in 1845.

George was 42 years old when his daughter, Lucrecia Ann, was born in 1846.

He was 47 years old when his brother, Frank, passed away in 1851. His son, William, was born the same year.

George was 57 years old when his daughter, Eliza, was born in 1861.

He was 63 years old when Ontario was founded on July 1, 1867.

George was 66 years old when his son, Thomas, passed away in 1870.

He was 69 years old when his sister, Margaret, passed away in 1873.

George was 72 years old when his daughter, Lucrecia, passed away in 1876.

He was 73 years old when his daughter, Eliza, passed away in 1877. Eliza was 16 years old.

George was 78 years old when he passed away in Bedford, Ontario in 1882. He is buried in Kingston, Ontario.

ANDREW HOWIE[54]

Andrew was born in 1870.

He was 12 years old when the mining boom in northern Ontario began in 1883.

Andrew was 24 years old when he married Lucy in Frontenac, Ontario on November 28, 1894.

He was 25 years old when his daughter, Dorcas, was born in 1896.

Andrew was 27 years old when his daughter, Ivy Rose Lee, was born in 1898.

He was 29 years old when his father passed away on July 8, 1900. His daughter, Lorraine Lucy, was born on August 14th.

Andrew was 35 years old when his son, Arlington Verlon Lloyd, was born in 1905.

He was 37 years old when his son, Noble Andrew, was born in 1908.

Andrew was 39 years old when his mother passed away in 1909.

He was 40 years old when his son, Harold Wallace Martin, was born in 1910.

Andrew was 62 years old when his brother, James, passed away in 1933.

He was 63 years old when he passed away in 1934. Andrew was Methodist.

LUCY AMERALLA CELISTINE (BRIDGE) HOWIE[55]

Lucy was born in 1870.

She was 11 years old when the Chinese Exclusion Act was passed in 1882.

Lucy was 19 years old when her sister, Ednie Florence Pearl, passed away in 1890.

She was 24 years old when she married Andrew in Frontenac, Ontario on November 28, 1894.

Lucy was 25 years old when her daughter, Dorcas May, was born in 1896.

She was 27 years old when her daughter, Ivy Rose Lee, was born in 1898.

Lucy was 30 years old when her daughter, Lorraine Lucy, was born in 1900.

She was 35 years old when her son, Arlington Vernon Lloyd, was born in 1905.

Lucy was 37 years old when her son, Noble Andrew, was born in 1908.

She was 39 years old when her son, Harold Wallace Martin, was born in 1910.

Lucy was 48 years old when her father passed away in 1919.

She was 63 years old when her husband passed away in 1934.

Lucy was 68 years old when her son, Harold, passed away in 1939.

She was 73 years old when her daughter, Lorraine, passed away on October 6, 1943. Her mother passed away on January 17, 1944.

Lucy was 75 years old when her brother, Barton Brewer, passed away in 1945.

She was 80 years old when she passed away in 1950. Lucy was Methodist.

ANNA A. HUDSON[56]

Anna served as a nurse in the military.
She passed away on March 19, 1951.

JAMES HUNTER[57]

James was born in 1857.

He was 10 years old when Ontario was founded on July 1, 1867.

James was 14 years old when British Columbia joined the confederation in 1871.

He was 60 years old when he passed away in 1917.

MARY ALIDA "IDA" (CONGER) HUNTER[58]

Ida was born in 1861. She was German.

She was five years old when Ontario was founded on July 1, 1867.

Ida was 21 years old when the mining boom in northern Ontario began in 1883.

She was 25 years old when she married James on February 19, 1887.

Ida was 42 years old when her mother passed away in 1904.

She was 44 years old when Ontario Hydro was established in 1906.

Ida was 45 years old when her father passed away in 1907.

She was 75 years old when the Neutrality Act was passed in 1937.

Ida was 77 years old when she passed away in 1939. She was Methodist.

CLARA MARGARET (WATSON) HYLAND[59]

Clara was born in Ontario on November 14, 1888 according to her death certificate although her gravestone says 1886.

She was 17 years old when Ontario Hydro was established in 1906.

Clara was 23 years old when she married Murton James in Peterborough, Ontario on September 24, 1912.

She was 28 years old when her father passed away in 1917.

Clara was 43 years old when she passed away in 1932. She was Irish.

DANIEL HYLAND[60]

Daniel passed away in Kingston, Frontenac, Canada West on March 7, 1857.

JANE ELEANOR (BELL) HYLAND[61]

Jane was born in 1859.

She was seven years old when Ontario was established on July 1, 1867.

Jane was nine years old when her brother, Albert Frederick, passed away in 1869.

She was 11 years old when British Columbia joined the confederation in 1871.

Jane was 22 years old when her brother, William Henry, passed away in 1882.

She was 23 years old when the mining boom in northern Ontario began in 1883.

Jane was 28 years old when her mother passed away in 1888.

She was 30 years old when the Women's Suffrage movement began in 1890.

Jane was 31 years old when she passed away on March 7, 1891.

JOHN HYLAND[62]

John was born in 1799.

He was 59 years old when he passed away in 1858.

MARY ANN (McDADE) HYLAND[63]

Mary Ann was born in 1801.

She was 57 years old when her husband passed away in 1858.

Mary Ann was 70 years old when British Columbia joined the confederation in 1871.

She was 75 years old when she passed away in 1876.

MARY ELLEN (McCARTEN) HYLAND[64]

Mary was born in 1796.

She was 51 years old when she passed away in 1847.

MURTON JAMES HYLAND[65]

Murton was born in Kingston Mills, Ontario on August 25, 1883. He was Irish.

He was 17 years old when his mother passed away in 1900.

Murton was 21 years old when he married Myrtle in Kingston, Ontario on November 9, 1903.

He was 24 years old when he married Clara in Peterborough, Ontario on September 24, 1912.

Murton was 39 years old when his father passed away in 1923.

He was 48 years old when his wife passed away in 1932.

Murton was 93 years old when he passed away in 1977.

[1] https://www.wikitree.com/genealogy/Guess-Family-Tree-674

[2] https://www.wikitree.com/genealogy/Guess-Family-Tree-830

[3] https://www.wikitree.com/genealogy/Hall-Family-Tree-64058

[4] https://www.wikitree.com/genealogy/Hansen-Family-Tree-20115

[5] https://www.wikitree.com/genealogy/Harback-Family-Tree-21

[6] https://www.wikitree.com/genealogy/Howie-Family-Tree-1493

[7] https://www.wikitree.com/genealogy/Harpell-Family-Tree-108

[8] https://www.wikitree.com/genealogy/Harpell-Family-Tree-109

[9] https://www.wikitree.com/genealogy/Harpell-Family-Tree-110

[10] https://www.wikitree.com/genealogy/Harpell-Family-Tree-111

[11] https://www.wikitree.com/genealogy/Harpell-Family-Tree-112

[12] https://www.wikitree.com/genealogy/Harpell-Family-Tree-113

[13] https://www.wikitree.com/genealogy/Johnson-Family-Tree-129346

[14] https://www.wikitree.com/genealogy/Harpell-Family-Tree-114

[15] https://www.wikitree.com/genealogy/Harpell-Family-Tree-115

[16] https://www.wikitree.com/genealogy/Harpell-Family-Tree-116

[17] https://www.wikitree.com/genealogy/Hatch-Family-Tree-6502

[18] https://www.wikitree.com/genealogy/Hayes-Family-Tree-20382

[19] https://www.wikitree.com/genealogy/Unknown-Family-Tree-625271

[20] https://www.wikitree.com/genealogy/Henderson-Family-Tree-27203

[21] https://www.wikitree.com/genealogy/Henderson-Family-Tree-27204

[22] https://www.wikitree.com/genealogy/Murray-Family-Tree-25794

[23] https://www.wikitree.com/genealogy/Hendry-Family-Tree-2535

[24] https://www.wikitree.com/genealogy/Hendry-Family-Tree-2541

[25] https://www.wikitree.com/genealogy/Hendry-Family-Tree-2543

[26] https://www.wikitree.com/genealogy/Hendry-Family-Tree-2544

[27] https://www.wikitree.com/genealogy/Harpell-Family-Tree-94

[28] https://www.wikitree.com/genealogy/Henry-Family-Tree-11840

[29] https://www.wikitree.com/genealogy/Henry-Family-Tree-11839

[30] https://www.wikitree.com/genealogy/Purdy-Family-Tree-3105

[31] https://www.wikitree.com/genealogy/Herkimer-Family-Tree-80

[32] https://www.wikitree.com/genealogy/McKegg-Family-Tree-33

[33] https://www.wikitree.com/genealogy/Smith-Family-Tree-290695

[34] https://www.wikitree.com/genealogy/Hogan-Family-Tree-6725

[35] https://www.wikitree.com/genealogy/Hogan-Family-Tree-6726

[36] https://www.wikitree.com/genealogy/McMillan-Family-Tree-6988

[37] https://www.wikitree.com/genealogy/Horning-Family-Tree-913

[38] https://www.wikitree.com/genealogy/Horning-Family-Tree-914

[39] https://www.wikitree.com/genealogy/Unknown-Family-Tree-625469

[40] https://www.wikitree.com/genealogy/Irvine-Family-Tree-6725

[41] https://www.wikitree.com/genealogy/McMillen-Family-Tree-1435

[42] https://www.wikitree.com/genealogy/Cranston-Family-Tree-979

[43] https://www.wikitree.com/genealogy/Horning-Family-Tree-915

[44] https://www.wikitree.com/genealogy/Horning-Family-Tree-916

[45] https://www.wikitree.com/genealogy/Benjamin-Family-Tree-4134

[46] https://www.wikitree.com/genealogy/Howard-Family-Tree-31485

[47] https://www.wikitree.com/genealogy/Connor-Family-Tree-4411

[48] https://www.wikitree.com/genealogy/VanOrden-Family-Tree-337

[49] https://www.wikitree.com/genealogy/Galloway-Family-Tree-4835

[50] https://www.wikitree.com/genealogy/Howe-Family-Tree-13944

[51] https://www.wikitree.com/genealogy/Howe-Family-Tree-2348

[52] https://www.wikitree.com/genealogy/Bennett-Family-Tree-36958

[53] https://www.wikitree.com/genealogy/Howes-Family-Tree-1403

[54] https://www.wikitree.com/genealogy/Howie-Family-Tree-1073

[55] https://www.wikitree.com/genealogy/Bridge-Family-Tree-1801

[56] https://www.wikitree.com/genealogy/Hudson-Family-Tree-16715

[57] https://www.wikitree.com/genealogy/Hunter-Family-Tree-23218

[58] https://www.wikitree.com/genealogy/Conger-Family-Tree-948

[59] https://www.wikitree.com/genealogy/Watson-Family-Tree-36737

[60] https://www.wikitree.com/genealogy/Hyland-Family-Tree-1725

[61] https://www.wikitree.com/genealogy/Bell-Family-Tree-39196

[62] https://www.wikitree.com/genealogy/Hyland-Family-Tree-1726

[63] https://www.wikitree.com/genealogy/McDade-Family-Tree-595

[64] https://www.wikitree.com/genealogy/McCarten-Family-Tree-69

[65] https://www.wikitree.com/genealogy/Hyland-Family-Tree-1171

Also by Angeline Gallant

A Dragon's Diary
Dreaming of Dragons

Calling Her Heart
Whisper of the Heart
No Turning Back
Forsake Me Not
Hear My Cry
Calling Her Heart Boxed Set Volumes 1-4

FORGET ME NOT
Victoria, Ontario's Babies 1894 - 1895

Keeper Of Secrets
A Lady's Secret

Midnight's Awakening

Heart of the Storm
Walking Through The Storm
Midnight's Awakening boxed set volumes 1-3

Secrets of the Underworld
Deklan's Dragons
Secrets of the Underworld Volumes 1 & 2

Tell My Story Collection
Tell My Story: England 1852

The Grave Whisperer
Wedding Bells in Kingston, Ontario, Canada 1923
St. Paul's Anglican Churchyard Kingston, Ontario, Canada A-B
St. Paul's Anglican Churchyard, Kingston, Ontario, Canada C - D
St. Paul's Anglican Churchyard, Kingston, Ontario, Canada G - H
St. Paul's Anglican Churchyard, Kingston, Ontario, Canada J - N
St. Paul's Anglican Churchyard, Kingston, Ontario, Canada O - R
St. Paul's Anglican Churchyard, Kingston, Ontario, Canada S - T
St. Paul's Anglican Churchyard, Kingston, Ontario T - Z
Small Graveyards & Burial Grounds: Kingston, Ontario, Canada
Cataraqui United Church Cemetery 1
Cataraqui United Church Cemetery 2
Cataraqui United Church Cemetary 3
Cataraqui United Church Cemetery 4
Cataraqui United Church Cemetery 5
Beth Israel Cemetery
Cataraqui United Church Cemetery 6

www.ingramcontent.com/pod-product-compliance
Lightning Source LLC
Chambersburg PA
CBHW052202150726
48002CB00003B/1092